South Carolina

Jim Ollhoff

Visit us at
www.abdopublishing.com

Published by ABDO Publishing Company, 8000 West 78th Street, Suite 310, Edina, Minnesota 55439 USA. Copyright ©2010 by Abdo Consulting Group, Inc. International copyrights reserved in all countries. No part of this book may be reproduced in any form without written permission from the publisher. The Checkerboard Library™ is a trademark and logo of ABDO Publishing Company.

Printed in the United States.

Editor: John Hamilton
Graphic Design: Sue Hamilton
Cover Illustration: Neil Klinepier
Cover Photo: iStock Photo

Manufactured with paper containing at least 10% post-consumer waste

Interior Photo Credits: Alamy, AP Images, Corbis, Getty, Granger Collection, iStock Photo, Jupiterimages, Library of Congress, Mile High Maps, Mountain High Maps, National Oceanic and Atmospheric Administration, One Mile Up, U.S. Army, U.S. Dept of Agriculture/Rob Flynn, and U.S. National Park Service/Carlin Timmons.
Statistics: State population statistics taken from 2008 U.S. Census Bureau estimates. City and town population statistics taken from July 1, 2007, U.S. Census Bureau estimates. Land and water area statistics taken from 2000 Census, U.S. Census Bureau.

Library of Congress Cataloging-in-Publication Data

Ollhoff, Jim.
  South Carolina / Jim Ollhoff.
     p. cm. -- (The United States)
  Includes index.
  ISBN 978-1-60453-676-8
  1. South Carolina--Juvenile literature. I. Title.

F269.3.O45 2010
975.7--dc22
                    2008052400

Table of Contents

The Palmetto State

South Carolina has long sandy beaches, beautiful mountains, and rich forests. It is a place known for its many golf courses. It is also a good place for music, theater, and the arts.

South Carolina is one of the 13 original colonies of the United States. It is a place of much important history. The first shots of the Civil War were fired in South Carolina.

South Carolina's nickname is "The Palmetto State." The palmetto is the state tree. It grows mostly along the coast. The palmetto appears on the state seal, the state flag, and even on South Carolina license plates.

South Carolina is known for its beautiful beaches and tall palmetto trees.

Quick Facts

Name: Named for England's King Charles I and King Charles II

State Capital: Columbia

Date of Statehood: May 23, 1788, the 8th state

Population: 4,479,800 (24th-most populous state)

Area (Total Land and Water): 31,113 square miles (80,582 sq km), 40th-largest state

Largest City: Columbia, population 124,818

Nickname: The Palmetto State

Motto: *Dum Spiro, Spero* (Latin for "While I breathe, I hope")

State Bird: Carolina Wren

State Flower: Yellow Jessamine

Blue Granite

Palmetto

Sassafras Mountain

Andrew Jackson

State Stone: Blue Granite

State Tree: Palmetto

State Song: "Carolina" and "South Carolina on My Mind"

Highest Point: Sassafras Mtn, 3,560 feet (1,085 m)

Lowest Point: 0 feet (0 m), Atlantic Ocean

Average July Temperature: 80˚F (27˚C)

Record High Temperature: 111˚F (44˚C) in Camden, June 28, 1954

Average January Temperature: 50˚F (10 ˚C)

Record Low Temperature: -19˚F (-28˚C) on Caesars Head, January 21, 1985

Average Annual Precipitation: 49 inches (124 cm)

Number of U.S. Senators: 2

Number of U.S. Representatives: 6

U.S. Presidents Born in South Carolina: Andrew Jackson

U.S. Postal Service Abbreviation: SC

Geography

The state of South Carolina is shaped like an upside-down triangle, with one point facing south. The Atlantic Ocean is to the east. The state of North Carolina is to the north. Georgia borders South

A railroad bridge crosses over the Savannah River between South Carolina and Georgia.

Carolina to the southwest. The Savannah River forms most of the border between Georgia and South Carolina. The Savannah River is 341 miles (549 km) long.

The northwest corner of South Carolina contains the Blue Ridge Mountains. This is part of the Appalachian Mountains, which stretch from Canada to Alabama. The highest point in South Carolina is Sassafras Mountain. It is in the Blue Ridge area.

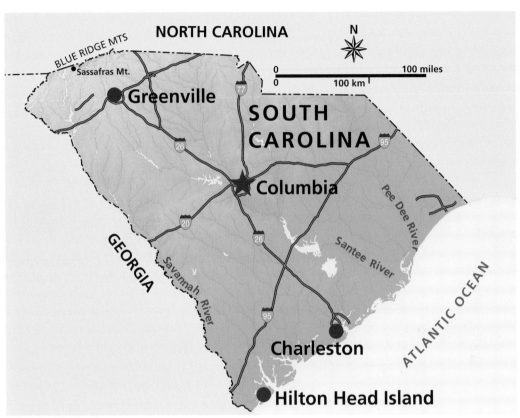

NORTH CAROLINA

N

BLUE RIDGE MTS

Sassafras Mt.

0   100 miles
0   100 km

Greenville

SOUTH CAROLINA

77

95

26

Columbia

20

GEORGIA

Savannah River

26

Pee Dee River

Santee River

ATLANTIC OCEAN

95

Charleston

Hilton Head Island

South Carolina's total land and water area is 31,113 square miles (80,582 sq km). It is the 40th-largest state. The state capital is Columbia.

Along the Atlantic Ocean coast, the land is called the coastal plain. This area is mostly flat, and has some marshes and

A flat, sandy beach on the coast of South Carolina.

sandy beaches. Some areas in the coastal plain are good for farming. Along the Atlantic Ocean, South Carolina has 187 miles (301 km) of coastline.

The coastal plain reaches about midway through the state, near Columbia. The area between the coastal plain and the Blue Ridge Mountains is called the Midlands, or the Piedmont. This area includes rolling hills, farmland, and forests.

Besides the Savannah River, South Carolina has two other important rivers. The Santee River is in the middle of the state. The Pee Dee River is in the northeast part of the state. It extends from the Atlantic Ocean up into North Carolina.

South Carolina does not have large natural lakes. Several artificial lakes have been created by putting dams on rivers.

Lake Murray was created when a dam was built on the Saluda River. The Lake Murray Dam was completed in 1930. At that time, it was the largest earthen dam in the world. Today, Lake Murray is 41 miles (66 km) long and 14 miles (23 km) wide. The land now beneath Lake Murray once held buildings and even a bridge, which can still be seen beneath its waters.

A sonar image of Wye's Ferry Bridge under Lake Murray.

Climate and Weather

South Carolina has hot and humid summers. The state is low and flat, so warm air from the Atlantic Ocean keeps the state warm and humid.

Winters are mild. The Appalachian Mountains to the west block winter air that freezes the Midwestern states.

In Columbia, South Carolina, average summer temperatures vary between 70 degrees Fahrenheit (21°C) and 92 degrees Fahrenheit (33°C). Winters in Columbia vary between 34 degrees Fahrenheit (1°C) and 57 degrees Fahrenheit (14°C).

In South Carolina, hurricanes can sometimes strike. These large storms come west off the Atlantic Ocean.

They get energy from warm southern waters. The worst hurricane to hit the state was in 1893. About 2,000 people died. In 1989, Hurricane Hugo caused about $7 billion in damage.

A satellite view of Hurricane Hugo headed towards South Carolina.

Boats are piled up on shore after Hurricane Hugo struck in 1989.

Plants and Animals

South Carolina was once almost entirely covered by forests. Today, about two-thirds is forested. The forests along the coast have trees such as oak, hickory, magnolia, longleaf, shortleaf, and loblolly. In the wetter, swampier areas, different kinds of trees grow. Cypress, tulip, sweet gum, and tupelo grow better in the marshy areas. Along the coast, the state tree, the palmetto, is common.

In the middle part of the state, shortleaf and loblolly pine are common. Oak, hickory, ash, and elm can also be found. In the Blue Ridge Mountains, in the northwest corner of the state, oak and hickory are common.

The Sabal palm, or palmetto, is the state tree of South Carolina. They can grow to heights of 90 feet (27 m), but usually grow 40-50 feet (12-15 m) in height. The trees are often found along the coast.

Wild Turkey

South Carolina has many white-tailed deer, rabbits, and raccoons. Red fox and wild pigs can also be found. Black bears are rarely seen in the state. Beavers and wild turkeys once were almost gone, but have made a comeback.

Alligators live along the coastal area of South Carolina. There are more than 40 different kinds of snakes, including 6 species of poisonous snakes. Frogs, toads, and the spotted salamander, the state amphibian, live in the swampy areas.

There are more than 350 different kinds of birds in South Carolina. These include mockingbirds, ducks, geese, pelicans, turkeys, herons, and egrets. The state bird is the Carolina wren.

American alligators are found in South Carolina.

Spotted Salamander

Pelican

Frog

History

Native Americans lived in South Carolina many years before Europeans arrived. These tribes included the Catawba, Cusabo, Cherokee, and Yamasee.

Spanish and French explorers came to explore the South Carolina area in the 1500s and 1600s.

Spaniard Francisco Gordillo explored the South Carolina area in 1521. Afterwards, Spain and France tried to settle the area. They failed because of disease, lack of food and supplies, and conflicts with Native Americans.

English settlers came in 1670. They set up the first successful European settlement. Their village was along the west bank of the Ashley River. About 10 years later, they moved their settlement across the river, to the area that is now Charleston.

South Carolina prospered under English rule. It had good trade, and exported furs, rice, and indigo. Charleston became an important city of the American colonies.

Indigo

Many Native Americans died from European diseases. Other Native Americans tried to defend their lands, but they were driven off by the settlers. Most of the Native American tribes had left the state by the 1770s.

In 1715, South Carolina's Governor Craven led an attack on the Yamasee Indians at the Combahee River.

The American colonies declared their independence from England in 1776. More than 200 Revolutionary War battles were fought in South Carolina.

The Battle of Cowpens, South Carolina, in 1781, was a victory for American soldiers over the British.

Large cotton plantations developed in the state. Many African American slaves were used to harvest the crops. The Civil War erupted in 1861. Shots were fired at Fort Sumter, in Charleston. This marked the beginning of the Civil War. South Carolina joined the Confederacy, a group of 11 Southern states that wanted to secede from the United States. These Southern states had large plantations and wanted to keep slavery legal.

On April 7, 1863, nine Union ironclad ships fought a great sea battle near Confederate-manned Fort Sumter, Charleston, South Carolina. Heavily out-gunned, the ironclads fought for two hours before retreating.

Many battles were fought on South Carolina soil. The state endured terrible destruction. Many cities were burned. Poverty was common for decades after the war ended in 1865.

Just as South Carolina's economy began to recover, more bad things happened. In 1886, a major earthquake struck the state, causing a lot of damage. In 1893, a hurricane killed 2,000 people. Then, during the 1920s, a beetle called the boll weevil destroyed much of the cotton in the state. In 1929, the Great Depression hit the United States. It was

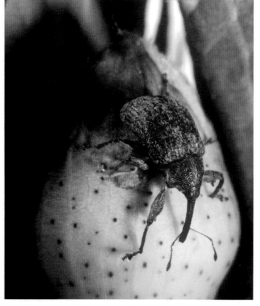

Boll weevils, arriving from South America, destroyed much of South Carolina's cotton crop in the 1920s. However, the bug is credited with forcing farmers to plant other crops, varying the products grown in the state.

a time when many people couldn't find jobs. The Great Depression hit South Carolina very hard.

The United States government spent money on new building programs during the Great Depression. Some of those, like the building of the Santee-Cooper Hydroelectric Project, benefited the people of South Carolina.

After World War II, state leaders convinced businesses to come to South Carolina. By the 1970s, South Carolina had military bases, industries, social services, centers for tourism, and many kinds of businesses. Over the years, South Carolina has made a strong economy for itself.

Aerial view of Camp Croft

Camp Croft Infantry Replacement Training Center (IRTC) was officially activated on January 10, 1941. Many World War II soldiers trained in this South Carolina facility. Closed in 1947, today parts of it are seen in Croft State Park.

Did You Know?

South Carolina got its name from kings.

The British were among the first Europeans to explore the area of North and South Carolina. They claimed the land. This meant that they believed they owned it, even though Native Americans had been living there for thousands of years.

In 1629, King Charles I of England gave

King Charles I

King Charles II

the land of North and South Carolina to Sir Robert Heath. In those days, the area was known as Carolus. This is a word from the Latin language, meaning "Charles." It was meant to honor King Charles I. King Charles II, the son of King Charles I, changed "Carolus" to "Carolina" in 1663. People began to refer to the south side of the area as "South Carolina." In the early 1700s, the British divided the land into two separate colonies, North Carolina and South Carolina.

People

Andrew Jackson (1767-1845) was the seventh president of the United States. He was born in Waxha, South Carolina. He went to college in North Carolina and then moved to Tennessee. He joined the military in the Revolutionary War, even though he was only 13 years old. He became a hero in the War of 1812 against the British. He was president from 1829-1837.

Sarah Grimke

Angelina Grimke Weld

Sarah Grimke (1792-1873) and her sister, **Angelina Grimke Weld** (1805-1879), were born in Charleston. They were abolitionists, which meant they were against slavery. They were born into a slaveholder's home, but grew to hate slavery. They gave many lectures and wrote many articles against slavery. Later, they became activists for women's rights, and spoke out against the poor treatment of women.

Dizzy Gillespie (1917-1993) was born in Cheraw, South Carolina. His given name was John Birks Gillespie, but he went by the name of "Dizzy" because he liked to clown around. He was one of the greatest jazz trumpet players of all time. He taught himself how to play the trombone, but then switched to trumpet at the age of 12. He was one of the founders of the style of jazz music called bebop. Later in life, he traveled the world to share his knowledge of music with young people.

James Brown (1933-2006) is often called the "Godfather of Soul" music. He was born in Barnwell, South Carolina. As a child, having moved to Georgia, neighbors taught him how to play musical instruments. He began singing and performing. He was very creative with his voice and body on stage. James Brown's abilities inspired a whole generation of performers. In 1986, he was inducted into the Rock and Roll Hall of Fame.

Joe Frazier (1944-) was born in Beaufort, South Carolina. He won a boxing gold medal in the 1964 Summer Olympic Games. He was the world heavyweight champ from 1970-1973. His most famous was a victory against Muhammad Ali in 1971. When he retired, Frazier's record was 32 wins, 4 losses, and 1 tie. After his retirement, he opened a gym to train young boxers. He wrote an autobiography called *Smokin' Joe*.

Cities

Columbia is the largest city in South Carolina. It has a population of 124,818. It is also the capital of the state, and a leading center for business. It began in 1786, when the South Carolina legislature wanted to create a town in the center of the state to be the new capital. The University of South Carolina is one of several colleges in the city.

Charleston

Charleston is a major port on the Atlantic Coast. It was settled by English colonists in 1670. It was first named "Charles Town," after King Charles II of England. In 1783, it became known as Charleston. The city's population is 110,015. More than half a million people live in the suburbs and surrounding area. Fort Sumter is in the Charleston area. It is famous as the place where the first shots of the Civil War were fired in 1861. The College of Charleston, founded in 1770, is also located there.

Greenville is near Spartanburg in the northwestern part of the state. The area was probably settled in the 1760s. The city was officially founded in 1831. It is near the Reedy River. This river was used to power manufacturing plants in the late 1800s. There are still many kinds of manufacturing facilities there, including cloth, chemicals, paper, machinery, and electronics. Greenville has a population of 58,754 people. When counting Spartanburg and all of the nearby towns, the population rises to almost a million people.

Hilton Head Island is the name of a town, and also the name of the island where the town sits. It is off the coast of the South Carolina mainland on the south side of the state. It is named for William Hilton. He was an English sea captain who saw the island in 1663. Originally, many settlers grew rice. Today, it is largely a resort community, with a population of 33,994.

Transportation

Interstate highways crisscross South Carolina. Interstates 85, 20, and 95 angle northeast and southwest across the state. Interstate 385

The Ashley River Bridge and Highway 17.

cuts across the state northwest to southeast. Interstate 77 goes north out of Columbia. State highways and freeways total 66,250 miles (106,619 km).

There are six major airports in South Carolina. The busiest is Charleston International Airport. The airports in South Carolina are smaller than the big airports in surrounding states.

Railroads in South Carolina were built as early as 1830. Many were damaged during the Civil War and were not rebuilt. Today there are about 2,300 miles (3,701 km) of railroad track. The railroads transport mainly chemicals, lumber, and paper products.

The Port of Charleston is one of the busiest ports in the United States. The Port of Georgetown is also important.

A cargo ship is loaded at the Port of Charleston.

Natural Resources

South Carolina has more than 25,000 farms. Farmers grow many kinds of crops, including soybeans, peaches, tobacco, cucumbers, and tomatoes. Farmers

also raise many turkeys, chickens, and dairy cows. Cotton was very important to the state in the 1800s, but became much less important in the 1900s. The agricultural industry in South Carolina brings in more than $2 billion each year to the state.

South Carolina is the only state east of the Mississippi River that mines gold. The state also mines sand, clay, gravel, stone, and gemstones.

Commercial fishing brings in about $25 million each year. The most important catches are shrimp, oysters, crabs, and clams.

Red Snapper caught by commercial fishermen in South Carolina. Most of these tasty fish are sold to restaurants.

Industry

In the 1700s and 1800s, agriculture was the most important industry in South Carolina. But by the early 1900s, manufactured goods became more

A worker in a textile mill. In the early 1900s, many South Carolina mills were built. Some are still in business.

important to the state's economy. South Carolina grew a lot of cotton in the late 1800s and early 1900s. Many factories were built that turned the cotton into clothing and other products. These products are called textiles. Today, textiles are still important, but other factories also make paper, machinery, and chemicals.

Beachgoers enjoy a sunny day at Pawley's Island, near Myrtle Beach, South Carolina.

After manufacturing, tourism is South Carolina's second-most important industry. Tourism in South Carolina includes great summer beaches and lots of golfing. Historic sites also bring in many tourists. Resorts are very popular. More than 30 million people come to South Carolina every year.

The United States military has several large bases in the state, including Shaw Air Force Base near Sumter, and the Marine Corps Recruit Depot Parris Island. These bases help support the state's economy.

Sports

The Carolina Panthers are a National Football League team. They represent both North and South Carolina, although the stadium is in North Carolina. South Carolina also has several minor league teams that play baseball, soccer, and ice hockey.

The Carolina Panthers' mascot, Sir Purr, leads the team onto the field.

College sports are very popular in the state. Clemson University and the University of South Carolina both have huge crowds at their football games.

NASCAR has held many races in South Carolina.

A NASCAR race at the Darlington Raceway.

Many races are held at the Darlington Raceway, near the city of Darlington, South Carolina.

For people who like the outdoors, there is plenty to do in South Carolina. The Atlantic Coast has swimming, fishing, and boating. The forests and mountains provide many places to hike and view nature. The state is also famous for its many golf courses.

Entertainment

There are many historic sites in South Carolina. Many honor events from the American Revolution and the Civil War. Cowpens National Battlefield and Kings Mountain National Military Park are near Gaffney. Fort Sumter National Monument in Charleston marks where the first battle of the Civil War was fought.

An aerial view of Fort Sumter.

A 42-pounder (19 kg) smoothbore cannon at Fort Sumter.

Charleston was one of the centers of art, music, and theater beginning in the early 1700s. The first opera in the United States was in Charleston in 1735. Many say the first theater in the United States opened in 1736 in Charleston. Orchestras were organized shortly after that.

The arts continue to be very important today in South Carolina. The Spoleto Festival USA is held in Charleston each year. It is a festival of performing arts, with music, dance, and theater.

Performers take the stage during the opening ceremonies of the Spoleto Festival USA, in Charleston, South Carolina.

Timeline

Pre-1500s—Native American tribes lived in the South Carolina area. The main tribes included the Catawba, Cusabo, Cherokee, and Yamasee.

1521—Spaniard Francisco Gordillo leads an expedition to the South Carolina area.

1670—The English begin a settlement near present-day Charleston.

1775—The start of the Revolutionary War. Many battles are fought in the state.

1861—The first shots of the Civil War are fired at Fort Sumter in Charleston.

Charleston in ruins.

1861-1865—South Carolina suffers much destruction during the Civil War.

1920s—The boll weevil destroys much of the state's cotton crop.

1929—The Great Depression begins. South Carolina's economy suffers.

1960s-1970s—The state's economy expands. Manufacturing and tourism become much more important.

1989—Hurricane Hugo hits South Carolina, causing $10 billion damage.

2003—South Carolina's Senator Strom Thurmond retires at age 100, after 48 years of service in the U.S. Senate.

Glossary

Blue Ridge Mountains—The mountain range in the northwest corner of the state.

Civil War—The war fought between America's Northern and Southern states from 1861-1865. The Southern states were for slavery. They wanted to start their own country. Northern states fought against slavery and a division of the country.

Coastal Plain—The low flat land near the ocean.

Confederacy—The Southern states of Alabama, Arkansas, Florida, Georgia, Louisiana, Mississippi, North Carolina, South Carolina, Tennessee, Texas, and Virginia. These states wanted to keep slavery legal. They broke away from the United States during the Civil War and formed their own country known as the Confederate States of America or just the Confederacy. The Confederacy ended in 1865, when the war ended and the 11 Confederate states rejoined the U.S.

Indigo—A tropical plant that is used to make a dark blue dye, which is often used to color cloth.

Marsh—A wet, swampy area.

Midlands—The name given to the land in the middle part of the state, between the coastal plain and the mountains.

NASCAR—National Association for Stock Car Auto Racing. A popular sporting event with races held across the United States. The Darlington Raceway, near the city of Darlington, hosts many NASCAR races.

Revolutionary War—The war fought between the American colonies and Great Britain from 1775-1783. It is also known as the War of Independence or the American Revolution.

Secede—To withdraw from a membership or alliance.

World War II—A conflict across the world, lasting from 1939- 1945. The United States entered the war in December 1941.

Index